MW00861796

Afterbirth

Cover art: Jennifer Watkins, "Afterbirth"
Interior design: Brianna Chapman and Jessie Truong
Editor: Jessie Truong
Publisher: Allison Blevins
Executive Editor: Kristiane Weeks-Rogers
Managing Editor: R. B. Simon

AFTERBIRTH
REBECCA MORTON
ISBN 978-1-957248-33-2
Harbor Editions,
an imprint of Small Harbor Publishing

Afterbirth

Rebecca Morton

Harbor Editions
Small Harbor Publishing

Contents

Afterbirth

Foster Care

After the presentation, we share breakfast: omelet,
potatoes, toast. My wife says, *I would.* Asks, *Would you?*

Scrambled, plastic bowls, when the social worker calls
at 6 am, two days early, *I'm bringing them now. Are you home?*

Cold bath, I think, when he falls that first week,
bloodied knees, gravel ground in.

We read humpty-dumpty only once: *This is
a stupid story*, she says, *Why was he up there?*

People ask, *Did you know? Without meeting them first?*
People ask, *Did you know? When you first met them?*

I whisk in cinnamon, vanilla, double drench the bread, but obviously
this ends in syrup. I'm always embarrassed by my own doubt.

I remember how my 2nd grade teacher cracked one
onto the asphalt. We stood in a circle, sun on our necks. Waited.

You Ask Why, Exactly, Your Birth Mom Left You (and What That Means About Love)

A sudden updraft plucks your kite from the grass,
string unspools until just one staple holds everything
in place. I don't know how to explain her mistakes.
I can tell you there's no competing with what rushes
in the vein. That's biology: a quick-patched
and porous breakwater. Once I watched
a red fox sprint across a freeway's six lanes.
Once I watched a square-jawed dog on a chain
make it halfway into the shade. You arrived in oversized
Spiderman tennis shoes. I've saved them in my closet
with files from the State. You can see how she tried.
And also, didn't try. Before you lead with anger: remember:
Each October we prune the hardy fuchsia to the ground
for overwintering, clean our shears and wait.
Eight months of deadwood and faith.

Adoption

All around me fallen toddlers scream until
adults pick them up. A mom asks, *Aren't you
sad about missing her first years?* I shake my head no.
No? She's sort of hollering at me. I explain I don't
look at it that way. She twists her mouth
into a pale frown, *I'd be very, very sad.* It is breezeless
here and the woodchips are weird, a sea
of landscaping material without any plants.
Someone told me foster kids are violent,
gerbil/garbage disposal situations. Someone
told me Russian orphans never bond. It's not humid,
but semi-muggy, kids run hot and the morning's
strange summer rain is puddled on hard surfaces.
The air smells like macerated cheddar crackers.
I've forgotten sunscreen so it's time to go.
Exiting, my toddler avoids her distraught peers,
suspicious of how they've beached themselves,
suspicious of assumptions about care.

> *she has your
> eyes she's tall is
> her mom tall define
> kin how did you
> choose her how
> did she arrive
> you missed morning
> sickness missed baby
> weight that's a
> blessing missed
> breastfeeding that's
> a shame you can
> only guess do you try
> to guess at her
> history you missed
> restless sleep a dark*

line an endless
shadow seam down
the belly

She was born into water then tacked to shore with a long thread through her thumb. In every roadside ravine stream I reached for a heel or something sturdy to wrench her from the silty water. She was barely breathing. She was a water-echo then a silent red cry.

You were in water and I was with you then.

Childbirth

At IKEA, we run into my son's friend Jack, and
while the boys rearrange strands of blinking
plastic stars, Jack's mom says, *I never would have
guessed foster care,* then asks, *Do you know much about
his mother.* To this landslide from decency, this
grit-scrubbed callus of pity, I ask, (twisting its
head into various awkward angles) if she knows
much about integrated LED goosenecks, I ask,
to this invasive thorny burr, this cuttlefish, if
she's swapped out all her incandescents yet, I ask
if internal-shelled sea chameleons prioritize
energy efficiency, and what light guides these
camouflaged goo cylinders as they swish about
the ocean floor, I ask if this lingonberry, this
reticent-to-bloom, slow growing, petite-leaved
groundcover prefers a wall mount sconce suckers
into the feathery red-burst coreopsis, I ask if

You Ask to Return Your Birth Mom's Gifts,
Won't Tell Me Why

Were you a sturdy, rubber-booted kid, did you learn to walk
in Searles Lake thick-muck ponds and brine pools hunting

crystals: trona, hanksite, borax used for laundry, used for shine.
Did you toddle, did you tug up fist-sized halite, pink in your pink

palms, razor-sharp, skin-smooth. Did you learn to talk tonguing
humidity and salt-caked teeth, lungs calibrated to a sulfur breeze,

Say rockhound say rockhound honey. Did you learn worth
in ashen mineral hauls, your mother a fly-by-night whimsy

with pockets full of prismatic gemstones, kneeling in the high-
sun chalk-colored sludge, her face so close you could see dusty

crow's feet, frown lines, misery, *These are yours these are for you,*
as she poured every glinting thing she had into your hands, poured

into your gray clay-clung hands more than you could ever hold.

Foster Care

what happens to

a spooked horse with a loosened pelham bit anxiety is a

thin   switch driving you how far how fast

wild-eyed   you flinched when I said *foster care* what's wrong with you

remember

foals that   we coaxed to the fence Wyoming's wild mustangs

follow me   under the red rock I'm unshod and shouldered-in

just like you when the storm comes

through   have you read

this poem   "Infertility" *You end me / like a period / / ends a sentence, /*

ends a line. / /

I don't know what biology's done to you

I know   some terrors won't relent and some animals

can run until their legs buckle under them

tonight   on my front stoop you're trembling with adrenaline

I am   not just a childhood friend I am your husband your

mother everyone you know *this will be*

my own   *my own child* you say over and over again

galloping

Foster Care

Hapless in my efforts, I throw my weight behind nurture
Here is a door, I offer, *Can't see it,* she replies
If you think love is boundless, let me tell you about
grief, which is boundless, too,
grief carried forward, a torch whip-stitched to her palm,
grief that wraps her up, sets her ablaze
If you don't believe in ghosts, let me tell you about
sliding paper-thin apple slices under her door,
I am here, I offer, *Can't see you,* she replies
Searching for grace, I become my hands
Washing her hair, I close my eyes to the smell of lavender

*

Mothering describes it as deep red, suckered to the umbilical cord, and pulsing. *Some people eat it*, I say to my wife, trying to show her the magazine one night in bed. Red dust, red earth, red sky, a wide bright field of red poppies, red tartan sweater my grandmother's hands mended, apple-red nail polish, three red cars in a row, red raincoats. My daughter's red raincoat. *Like an animal*, I say and dogear the map of it.

*

*

Do you ever wonder what she was like as an infant, a playground mom says as we trot over to our toddlers who are aggressively kicking-up wood chips. *I have some ideas,* I joke, as I drop to my knees.

*

*

Horses will. Maiden mares are more likely. *Eww,* ThoroughbredVT posts on the discussion board when it becomes clear that one of her mares ate the whole thing, and fast. *It's natural,* many respond.

*

*

Use a small, sharp knife. Carefully separate gristle and ligament. Refrigerate.

*

*

A friend sends me a picture of hers. More bruise-purple, more maroon, than red. Muscle-heavy if I held it in my hands, rivulets of plump veins if I pressed my thumbs in. Slick with thin bright blood, surgical scissors still clipped onto the cord's end. *What are you looking for?* She asks.

*

*

Sometimes it grows through the uterine wall, into uterine muscle, wraps itself around close-by organs. *Too attached*, *Mothering* says.

*

*

Add the tender parts to a simple bone broth and simmer until brown. Dry then crush into dust for capsules. Pickle in a Ball jar. Sauté with butter, onions. Spread thinly onto toast.

*

*

In Salvador Dalí's painting, a slight, deep-red-rimmed red pool rests outside the person-egg, a grotesque person-arm clawing out. *No*, I complain to a friend. *It should be purple and with veins.* My friend nods. *It should be enormous,* I say, *It's all wrong.*

*

*

Did the playground mom whipstitch a
velvet bag for her lotus birth, the baby
attached for five days by blue cord. Did
she watch it wither, break.

*

My mother, my aunt, my aunt in her green
and yellow ruffled blouse, my cousin at 16,
my cousin at 18, my daughter's birth mom.

*

My daughter's birth mom holding out a pink-frosted cupcake. Two white-flame candles blurring a toddler's quiet face. M—, When you returned, I rattled open, *my* I said, *mine* I said, but I was wrong: each minute she spent with you was a tethered, pulsing vein.

*

*

How can I answer? I am trying to imagine bringing it close. I smooth my palm along my belly, think of the Copper River salmon running now. Filled with translucent-orange roe. I practice opening and closing my mouth.

*

Childbirth

it was a blood-violet dream
in my horse-mind then
when I was to clamp the cord
press her to me
when I was to bleed out
cradle the head
milk-feed
it was a violet-cry
when I was to
prick the heel
lift her by crimson-clenched fists
clear the sigh
it was milk-blood then
when I was to wake at
each gurgle spit
when I was to low-sing
at each clenched-cry
(my body has no kin
stands with the horses
no crimson
I didn't violet
I didn't milk-sigh
there's no blood-sway
no baby

)

Foster Care

patience every minute spent gently unknotting snarled-in hairties is worth it *biology* a wisp-green tip of winter-sown lettuce in morning frost *biology* not the wide stone my spade keeps hitting *love* and what of its muddy landscape I can't find you everyone told me you'd be a small clear pool were those lies or am I failing *failure* I am not a flash of kindling not doubled-over flushed with rage *failure* how can I see a brushfire before it crests the berm *trauma* I recognize it I won't look away *love* and what of its muddy landscape I can't find you everyone told me you'd be a small clear pool were those lies or am I failing *biology* a wisp-green tip of winter-sown lettuce in morning frost not the wide stone my spade keeps hitting *love* a wisp-green tip of winter-sown lettuce in morning frost not the wide stone my spade keeps hitting *love* I am not a flash of kindling not doubled-over flushed with rage *love* every minute spent gently unknotting snarled-in hairties is worth it *love* I recognize it I won't look away *failure* I am not a flash of kindling not doubled-over flushed with rage *trauma* I recognize it I won't look away *love* and what of its muddy landscape I can't find you everyone told me you'd be a small clear pool were those lies or am I failing *failure* I am not a flash of kindling not doubled-over flushed with rage *failure* I am not a flash of kindling not doubled-over flushed with rage *failure* I am not a flash of kindling not doubled-over flushed with rage *failure* I am not a flash of kindling not doubled-over flushed with rage *failure* I am not a flash of kindling not doubled-over flushed with rage *failure* I am not a flash of kindling not doubled-over flushed with rage *failure* I am not a flash of kindling not doubled-over flushed with rage *failure* I am not a flash of kindling not doubled-over flushed with rage *failure* I am not a flash of kindling not doubled-over flushed with rage *failure* I am not a flash of kindling not doubled-over flushed with rage *failure* I am not a flash of kindling not doubled-over flushed with rage *failure* I am not a flash of kindling not doubled-over flushed with rage *failure* I am not a flash of kindling not doubled-over flushed

You Ask Your Birth Mom What Her Favorite Color Is (You've Never Asked Me That Question)

the chokecherry
onto which a beak
clamps feather edges
of a thousand cedar
waxwing flocks each
flock a thousand cat-
eyed birds mudrooms
you've clattered through
afraid to unsnap your
coat your coat except
the worn-out pockets
and elastic cuffs the skin
of grapes your birth
mom peels with her
front teeth childbirth
when bleeding won't
subside all the blood
my cupped palms
can hold that each
month removes
itself from me
the madrone falling
apart knot curled
into the core the skin
of red grapes you
peel like that too

Adoption

After Laura Read

The desert is an obvious stand-in for grief, which is why
I'm so familiar with Wyoming. Also, I have this old

View-Master that details the horizon's early morning light,
a sandstone canyon's spectrum of reds. Why a desert?

Vast is a partial answer. *Perpetual* another.
There are similar places, of course, I have walked

many dry lakebeds with their sorrows, but it is only
the desert's smooth-bellied occupants, coils of poison trills,

that hide in the plains of sagebrush. Some nights
I dream of you, your small, sticky hands

moving my pencils and cell phone about my desk.
Not now, I say, *I'm trying to work,* so you hover there,

holding crayoned and glued construction paper,
for hours. Or maybe these are memories.

What I hope for is probably impossible: to never return
to that desolate, mid-western town where,

even in winter, my mother would leave me in the car
when retrieving certain prescriptions from the drug store.

Turtled in my yellow puffy coat, breath filling
the backseat, I'd close my eyes to the crunch of tires

in icy slush. I learned about frostbite again
when your elastic bracelet strung with glitter-beads

disappeared deep in April's curb-piled snow.
I watched you fish around in that cold gray soup

too long. Called you inside too late. You struggled
as I peeled off all your sopping layers,

It's lost forever! you cried, your swollen hands
a brilliant spectrum of reds, and burning.

Advance Praise

In *Afterbirth* we meet a speaker who turns toward wonder and love, with vulnerable intention, to welcome the hard work of building a family. Rebecca Morton's poetry appeals to the gut, the brain, and the ear—sound rounds the corners of lines; revulsion shifts into curiosity; the narrative is rich with the music of repetition and vivid pastoral color. Sonnet, prose form, and experimental contrapuntal show us a heart so pulsing and raw that it creates a whole new blood-organ for nourishment and connection. Devour it.

Lynne Ellis, editor at Tulipwood Books and author of *Future Sketchbook*

Through lush language and irresistible equine sensibilities, Rebecca Morton reinforces the vulnerable line connecting mother and child. Her tether draws each of us closer, tugging at our every heart string, regardless of our family of origin. *Afterbirth* is sustenance for us all.

Kalehua Kim, author of *Mele*, Winner of the 2024 Trio House Press Editor's Choice Prize

Afterbirth gives the reader a window into the ways family can be uniquely created and defined. Morton's vivid descriptions, powerful language, and piercing concision weave together a satiating read. For anyone ruminating on mothering and the raising of children, *Afterbirth* is a compelling companion in the journey.

Erin Armstrong, recent work at Mom Egg Review, Exsolutas Press, and Indy Correspondent

Acknowledgments

Many thanks to the following journals where these poems first appeared, often in earlier versions:

Atlanta Review: "You Ask Why, Exactly, Your Birth Mom Left You (and What That Means About Love)"

Birdcoat Quarterly: "Adoption" [The desert is an obvious stand-in for grief, which is why]

CALYX: "Foster Care" [Hapless in my efforts, I throw my weight behind nurture]

The Cincinnati Review: "Adoption" [All around me fallen toddlers scream until]

Crab Creek Review: "You Ask to Return Your Birth Mom's Gifts, Won't Tell Me Why"

Cream City Review: "*"

Pacifica Literary Review: "You Ask Your Birth Mom What Her Favorite Color Is (You've Never Asked Me That Question)"

Appearance in "Foster Care" (7), "Infertility" by Wendy Chin-Tanner, "Poem-a-Day" (September 24, 2019), *the Academy of American Poets.*

Rebecca Morton's work appears in *The Offing*, *CALYX*, *Sugar House Review*, *RHINO*, *TriQuarterly*, *The Cincinnati Review*, *Pacifica Literary Review*, *Poetry Northwest* and elsewhere, and has been featured on *Verse Daily*. She serves as a poetry reader for *The Adroit Journal*, and holds an MFA in poetry from Eastern Washington University. Rebecca lives in Chicago with her wife and children.

About Small Harbor Publishing

Small Harbor Publishing is a 501c3 nonprofit organization. Our goal is to publish unique and diverse voices. We are a feminist press, and we are committed to diversity and inclusion. We strive to bring new voices to a devoted and expanding readership.

Small Harbor Publishing began in 2018 with the first issue of *Harbor Review*. The magazine is an online space where poetry and art converse. *Harbor Review* quickly grew and now publishes reviews and runs multiple micro chapbook competitions, including the Washburn Prize and the Editor's Prize.

In July 2020, Small Harbor Publishing was officially incorporated and began Harbor Editions. Harbor Editions accepts submissions through a chapbook open reading period, a hybrid chapbook open reading period, the Marginalia Series, and the Laureate Prize.

In 2023, Harbor Anthologies began with a mission to promote texts that explore social justice issues and highlight marginalized writers.

If you would like to support Small Harbor Publishing, please visit our "About" page at smallharborpublishing.com/about.